MW01593566

SEASONS OF GRIEF AND HOPE

A Reflective Journey through Quilts and Poetry

Monique Cerundolo

ISBN: 1492728144
ISBN-13: 978-1492728146

DEDICATION

To my husband Peter,
and my children Jeanine, Michael and Nicole

To Abuela, my grandmother and friend
and Stephen DeMott, MM,
whose faithful friendship inspired this book

CONTENTS

Acknowledgments   vii

1   Prologue   Pg #2

2   Winter   Pg #10

3   Autumn   Pg #22

4   Spring   Pg #32

5   Summer   Pg #38

6   Rising Anew   Pg #48

7   Seasons of Grief and Hope   Pg #52

8   Personal Reflection   Pg #56

9   Bibliography and Resources   Pg #60

ACKNOWLEDGMENTS

I started sharing "Seasons of Grief and Hope" in 2009 at Boston College, as part of my artistic Masters synthesis in Pastoral Ministry. This particular project required a theoretical piece and an exhibit presentation that explored and explained the power of art to elicit, express and contain feelings, and to educate and establish relationship in the context of the process of grief.

Throughout the process of creating and writing, my advisors and dear professors John Mc Dargh, Colleen Griffith and John Shea encouraged me, expanded my vision, and cheered the quilts and poetry that emerged. I am so grateful for their faithful companioning in this time of grief, hope, and healing. To them I also owe the new title and form of the project as they challenged me to develop and trust my grief journey through the seasons.

Friends and family participated in the first presentation and lovingly supported me through its creation and the many later exhibits with their understanding and encouragement, with their critique and counsel. To them I gratefully dedicate this book and its message of hope through the difficult times and especially the times of loss. My brother Alain, contributed his expertise in photography so that the quilts in the book would comply with publishing requirements. My friends Jane, Bill, Mary and Diana gave me crucial feedback on the manuscript in addition to their deep and reliable listening. Tmira walked with me through the ups and downs of grief and many challenging times. To my parents, I am grateful for their encouraging message "to write always."And to Steve DeMott, who enthusiastically exclaimed: "Monique, the world needs poets. Keep writing."

Since the first exhibit, many asked me to seriously consider sharing this in a broader way through publishing. Thank you to all who have told me time and again: "please make this into a book" and all those who wrote letting me know how this exhibit had moved them. To my dear colleague Chaplain Enos, I thank for his challenging me with: "and when are you going to do this?" His question moved me into finally engaging with this long delayed project.

I am grateful to those who hosted "Seasons of Grief and Hope" for their gracious welcoming and enthusiastic reception of it. They were also instrumental in this present effort. Thank you as well to the editors and staff of Create Space who have made this book possible.

Prologue

On March 31 of 2006, I lost one of my dearest friends. Steve was a Nebraska born Maryknoll missionary priest residing in Lima, Peru. We had met briefly at the Maryknoll residence during a two week immersion trip where my oldest children, then 14 and 16, and I shared the daily lives of poor and orphan children in two homes in the slums of Lima.

Though many thousand miles apart, Steve and I continued corresponding regularly when I returned home, and even got a chance to see each other a few times. Our friendship deepened as we shared stories from our ministries and as we walked through his sister's illness and death, and his second and third struggles with cancer. Unfortunately, though he fought bravely, he lost his battle to brain cancer. For ten months we talked openly about his imminent death and shared our sorrow, our hope, our joys and gratefulness for every moment life gave him and for our friendship. During the time of our waiting, and his battling with illness, I often found myself seeking refuge in poetry writing and quilting.

My desire is that, in viewing quilted nature scenes and reading poems that depict each season of this complex process, others can walk along their grief in hope. Through recognition of their own seasons of grief there may arise a sense that they are not walking this way alone. In addition, I would hope that, in the midst of their pain, they might also find a God who walks beside them, holding them every step of the way.

On Grief

We all carry a suitcase of grief. Whether we work caring for the sick and dying, tend to a dying relative, or find ourselves suddenly exiled from our everyday lives and faced with serious loss, illness or imminent death, grief is a lifelong companion, a reliable reality. Grieving well requires an active stance, a willingness to acknowledge our losses, to search for meaning, to reassess our life as we knew it, and find a constructive and enriching way to go forward. We don't get "over" grief, we have to get "through" it, by acknowledging and sharing our feelings, remembering, recognizing our loss, reflecting, expressing our sorrow, reaching out to others and re-orienting our lives.

We might helpfully define grief as: "... the normal but bewildering cluster of ordinary human emotions arising in response to a significant loss, intensified and complicated by the relationship to the person or object lost." (Mitchell and Anderson, 1983)

Since emotions are easier to illustrate through images, color and metaphors than tasks of grieving, I have selected the flow and color changes of the seasons for this journey.

It is best to imagine grief as a spiral staircase, rather than a straight line through predictable phases. Many occasions cause grief feelings to re-emerge: special holidays, anniversaries of the loss, special places. Losses tend to cumulate, and a new grief often brings up the previous ones to the surface. We may respond differently to different losses because each of our relationships has unique traits. The grief feelings will depend on the depth and quality of the relationship and the situation around each particular loss.

Suffering and Hope

Life crises stop us in our tracks. Our old ways of making meaning cease to work. Quite often, our very faith which should sustain us falters.

Struggle and pain challenge us by forcing us to stretch our spirit. In her book "Scarred by Struggle, Transformed by Hope" Joan Chittister (2005) states that each component of struggle opens the possibility of a gift: the process of struggle is counterbalanced by the process of hope. In this way, change can lead to a conversion of heart; isolation, to the gift of independence; darkness may strengthen our faith making it tried and true; fear can be overcome with renewed courage; powerlessness can bring the gift of surrender in trust; vulnerability, the gift of knowing one's limitations; exhaustion, the gift of endurance and resilience; and scarring, the gift of inner transformation.

Grief is a painful process where we wrestle with guilt and anger, looking for answers, resisting change, wracked with doubt, crushed by despair, but hoping against all hope to see the light of a new day. While we may feel completely abandoned by God during this time, God's love is active in the silence of our hearts, transforming and stretching us as we deal with the loss and find new direction in our lives.

Image

As I selected a scene to illustrate each poem, I tried to capture the feelings expressed metaphorically into colors and texture. Color and symbols (a swan, a lighthouse, a boat, rocks, water) complement a scene which, through starkness, stillness, cold or warm tones or movement, invites the viewer to enter emotionally into each artistic piece.

Images serve as catalysts for the process of grief through symbolism, evoking and bringing to awareness the strong emotions they elicit, inviting shared expression and relationship. They can provide the quiet and safe space one needs to reflect on and express the overwhelming set of feelings in the process of grief.

Grief is deeply personal and the journey takes different turns. An image helps us to recognize the feelings that overcome us at a particular time.

Healing

For me, to be with nature, to sift through swatches of colorful fabric and to pour feelings in verse, has been restoring. I realized that there is a healing aspect to making and offering a visual journey of this very personal yet quite universal path through grief.

In viewing, reading, reflecting, remembering and sharing, one begins to rebuild the shattered pieces of oneself. Through this visual journey of poetry, quilts and Biblical messages of sorrow and hope, this project intends to assist those grieving to take a more active stance in their path through grief, to connect to others, to find meaning in the midst of suffering, and healing in their pain.

Seasons of Grief and Hope

The journey...

This journey moves from the coldest and starkest of seasons to the warmest and most lush, thus re-arranging the seasons to suit the purpose of this project. Each season reflects a group of emotions that are part of the process of grief reminding us that the feelings are cyclical, re-emerging at different times and in different situations. Throughout the journey hope remains a constant thread and light as the seasons move us toward a new place or a new beginning. In addition, tasks of grief defined by Joyce Rupp (*Praying our Goodbyes*, 1990) are suggested as a reminder that this process is an active one. This is a time for remembering and reflecting on one's loss, recognizing its impact and meaning in our lives, finding a ritual that connects us with others and brings about a new relationship with the subject of our loss, and re-investing ourselves with new purpose and wisdom.

Winter:

Denial, numbness, disbelief, loneliness, emptiness, isolation, anger, sadness.

Autumn:

Fear and anxiety, guilt and shame, bargaining, longing, searching.

Spring

Sadness and depression, yearning.

Summer

Acceptance, integration of loss, re-orienting, new hope.

Take a moment to quiet yourself as you prepare to walk this Journey.

Allow the quilts to draw you in, enter them. At first, you may want to walk the journey from beginning to end. Later, you may return to the quilt or verse that moved you more deeply as this is the one that may be speaking to you at this time. As you walk this journey, read the poems slowly, you may even consider reading them aloud. Most importantly, take the time to stay with each image and to reflect on the feelings both image and verse elicit in you. As you walk this journey, you may keep the questions below in mind without feeling the need to answer them; these are here to guide your reflection, hopefully helping you to notice. At the end of the book, I suggest some questions for journaling or sharing within a group.

Which quilt captures your attention? Which word stays with you?

What mood do the picture and poem express to you? What feelings do they bring forth?

What do the colors and symbols suggest to you?

Is there a place of light in each quilt, or poem that speaks of hope to you?

What memories are brought forth by the quilts and poems?

How does this overall visual expression of grief touch you?

It is my hope that these pieces be viewed in a reflective way, as windows to the mystery and the sacred in our lives.

Each quilted piece and poem can then suggest metaphors of life and death, of light and darkness, of hope and despair, of anger and peace, and most of all of the Love that abides with us through it all, connecting us to others.

In walking slowly along this visual journey of grief the viewer is led from darkness and turmoil to renewed light and hope.

MONIQUE CERUNDOLO

WINTER

"I have dealt with great things that I do not understand." (Job 42: 3)

Tasks of grieving: *Remembering, Recognizing (the loss), Reflecting, Ritualizing and Re-orienting (our lives and hope)*

Shift

How does one walk
with just one leg?
How does one shift
one's weight?
How does one choose
to lose a piece of self?
-A leg, or death-
"Are you in pain?"
"Yes"
"I am sorry"
Silence stretched
and throbbed
around us.
Bewilderment
(I never imagined
it would hurt like this)
"I would like some ice chips"
To cool, to calm, to numb?
And when he gets them,
I wait, and watch,
as he torments the silence
crunching
chip after chip.
What can one say,
when one can feel
another's suffering?
"What helps you
now, to go through this?"
*"**Nothing**"*
Tinted with anger,
final
(I never asked for this).
I have no words of comfort
no pocket wisdom.
"I want to sit (like always)
on a chair"
(dangle my legs
down to the floor,
-did I say "legs"?).
And for a moment
I am in his place
and my heart aches
as intensely
as his missing leg.

"Winter"

Inner Snow

The clouds moan the birth of snow.
Branches slash a swollen sky
in stiffened plea.
A daze of blurry trees
and roofs now wan,
numbly awaits
the impending torment.

Why does this grief cling
to frozen pastures,
to unrippled waters
of a far away lake,
or seep, through oblivious pores,
To the bottom
of an endless pit?

Shoulders and brows
fail to admit
the tension of a drum
unraveled into heartbeats,
or the shivering
of skin whipped
by the wind.
It hurts outside. Inside, it snows.

"Alone"

"My God, my God, why have you abandoned me? . . . My God, I call by day, but you do not answer; by night, but I have no relief." (Psalm 22: 2a- 3)

Shades of Purple

I'd like to draw
every sharp corner
and dark recess
the subtle contour
of a sigh

I'd like to brush
the purple strokes
of sorrow
with silver water
and lavender snow

And then explore
crease after crease
every rough edge
of caves
molded by absence

"Frigid Morning"

"Lord, my God, I call out by day; at night I cry aloud in your presence. Let my prayer come before you; incline your ear to my cry." (Psalm 68: 2-3)

Grief

When will this river
end its flow?
And if it does,
how will the wavering pain
emerge again?

I hear the distant
rumbling of the ocean,
of far away waves
crashing onto
vanishing rocks.

The wind caresses
with a frigid hand.
The gulls cackle
their fish gossip.

It's lonesome here.
Solitude suits me these days.
The gray rocks face a gray sea
under a still grayer sky.

It's dark inside.
No one can walk
this way with me.
Not even God.

"Sorrow"

"All who call upon me I will answer, I will be with them in distress." (Psalm 91: 15a)

Longing

*Where do You dwell
elusive and impalpable,
invisible and concealed?*

*I Am.
In the sudden hush
amidst the noise of life,
in the ocean's tide
and the sharp white crests
of waves breaking wild.*

*I Am.
In the soft caress
of a cool evening breeze,
the refreshing shower
of a summer night,
and the wonder of a shooting star.*

*I Am.
In the whisper
of a passing wind,
the comforting words
of a faithful friend,
the music of a glorious hymn.*

*I Am.
In the joyful twinkle
of a child's bright eyes.
And most of all,
in the deepest corners
of your yearning soul.*

AUTUMN

"Autumn"

Tasks of grieving: Remembering, Recognizing (the loss), Reflecting, Ritualizing and Re-orienting (our lives and hope)

Towards the Light

How hard it is
to understand
the enveloping
darkness
when we walk, awkwardly,
                        towards the Light.

How hard it is
to accept the sting,
the bitter taste,
the ache
of our weary journey
                        towards the Light.

How hard it is
to answer "Yes"
when we suffer,
stumbling
-hesitant and frightened,-
                        towards the Light.

How hard it is
to take within
the awesome splendor,
the blaze,
the dazzling brightness
                        of God's Light.

"In the Storm"

"He woke up and rebuked the wind, and said to the sea: 'Quiet! Be still!' The wind ceased and there was great calm." (Mark 4: 35-40)

Life's Flows

The waves' earlier strokes
have become harsher
at high tide.
The surf seems
more determined now,
even brusque,
slapping the face of rocks
then retrieving new energy
for the next blow.
Water may seem meeker
than stone
but the scars left by glaciers
tell a different truth.
The ocean's force
bears down the stubborn
stiffness of granite.
In this battle,
David defeats Goliath
and the outcome is sand.
The strength of the weak is
to know
the weakness of the strong.
The waves are patient,
chipping their foe
one fragment at a time.
Their persistent pounding
has eternity on its side.
The unmoving rocks have no means
to fight the forceful flow,
no place to flee,
no power to retaliate.
...I'd like to have the strength
of water
against the rocks of life...

"Autumn Light"

"Darkness is not dark for you, and night shines as the day. Darkness and light are but one."
(Psalm 139: 12)

Light and Shadows

The earth hides beneath
an early morning haze
where fuzzy yellows gleam
against ever greening yews.
A spider web strings
beads of shimmering dew
-sturdy hammock
for a crafty acrobat-.
A gleeful chirp greets dawn,
clamors hunger, owns a tree.

Nature opens its hands
expansive, eager,
relishing in the stirring
rhythms of life.
The grip of early mist
wraps so tightly as to
suggest a certain substance.

Day breaks in diffused light
and faintly shadows.
Life swings to the edges
of dusk and dawn,
of murky waters
and clear streams,
of time both fleeting
and without end.

Light and shadows intertwined
dancing
in the fluid stillness
of our being.

"Canyons of Silence"

Sentinels of Time

Sentinels of time,
vessels of ages past.
Jagged whim
of boulders,
and huddled
domes,
the canyons stand.

At the brink of time,
earth cradles the river
of birth
and death.
Our lives glide by,
a flicker.
The canyons stand.

The Bridge of Knowing

Here,
at the end of time,
I stand between eternity
and now,
filled with dread.

I walk
by the river's edge.
Turbulent waters
drag moss,
pebbles, dreams.

A cliff
opens beneath my feet:
unknown depths
engulf
all that is.

The river,
the abyss await,
they guard the inescapable
secret
of our destiny.

I stop
at the beckoning gorge,
I pause at the river's rage,
and yearn,
I yearn for a bridge.

SPRING

"Spring Blossoms"

"I have called you by name: you are mine." (Isaiah 43: 1)

Tasks of grieving: *Remembering, Recognizing (the loss), Reflecting, Ritualizing and Re-orienting (our lives and hope)*

Yearning

Pangs of longing stretch
into the morning air:
futile attempts
to recover
what was lost.
Threads of memory
lace words into knots
of once shared meaning.
Bird song greets the sun
waking me to joy
and sadness.
Their call
pins me to the present,
flings me to the past.
Grief resides
in the present yearning,
the hollow place
left by someone dear
now gone.
Unawares,
spring bursts through
all its seams:
a yellow promise
of forsythias,
the exuberant energy
of tulips,
the uncomplicated
purple wisdom of pansies.
And the bird song:
the joyful clamor of starlings
the rapture of cardinals,
the plump red breasted
presence of robins.
Sadness seems out of place
in the midst of all this bliss.
Yet, it is here, lingering,
wrapping its vines
around my trunk.

"Spring"

Goodbye

How can this day
painfully glow with
such green cheer, when haze
has just moved in?

How can the sun
paint warmth on
crimson leaves with
only strokes of gray?

The colored shrubs,
the starlings' sass
the crickets' din, echo
a message in the wind.

...Goodbye...
Not fully uttered,
dangling unmoved,
burning as frosty air.

SUMMER

"Summer"

Tasks of grieving: *Remembering, Recognizing (the loss), Reflecting, Ritualizing and Re-orienting (our lives and hope)*

39

A Time to Build

"There is an appointed time for everything . . .
A time to be born, and a time to die;
a time to weep, and a time to laugh;
. . . a time to mourn and a time to dance."
(Ecclesiastes 3: 1, 2, 4)

"Flowing"

"When I was being made in secret, fashioned as in the depths of the earth. Your eyes foresaw my actions in your book all are written down; my days were shaped before I came to be." (Psalm 139: 15b-16)

Parting

I will remember you
in bird song
in winter frost
in starry nights.

I will remember you
in songs of praise,
in broken bread,
each time I pray.

A part of me
has gone with you,
a part of you
lives on with me.

I will remember you
in laughter shared,
in faith and sorrow too.
and I will thank our God
for the gift of you.

"Come and See"

" 'Rabbi, where are you staying?' He said to them,
'Come and you will see.' " (John 1: 38-39)

A Time to Build

After the storm,
the silence.
After the night,
breaks dawn.
Darkness is pierced
by sunlight,
moonlight
and the gleam
of infinite
luminous stars.
Day breaks along
a glimpse of hope,
its dew refreshing
the remains
of self.

"New Hope"

"And behold, I am with you always, until the end of the age." (Matthew 28: 20)

Haven

A winding path,
curling whimsically
between ancient trees,
lures me to follow
to places yet unknown.
It is here
where peace dwells:
in green leaves
and morning dew,
in fluttering wings
and humming birds,
in gentle sway
of branches in the breeze.
Joy abounds, exuding
in droplets that cling
to each blade of grass,
in a spider's web
and on pebbles crunching
beneath my feet.
Time has frozen here,
between leaps of deer
and scurrying hare,
in the still dawning
of a bright new day.

"Rising Anew"

Rising Anew

I Am

I hold hope with my fingers,
I hold a joy that lingers
in the scent of a rose
or a sunflower's warmth.
I hold the days of autumn,
I hold the winter snows.
I hold the moon, the fire,
and even the sun, at dawn.

Everything belongs to me:
through every pore I sip
the elusive time, the wind,
the love and the newborn's grin.
I possess a clear vision,
a keen taste, and the laughter
of a mountain river
which flows and sings.

I hold anguish beneath my skin,
a wavering dread that feigns
uncertain security.
I hold the smell of woods,
the sound of rivers,
the song of birds,
and lost tears running
on flushed red cheeks.

I am all that surrounds me,
what enters without my consent,
what grows in a subtle breath;
parts of me spread around the world
spilled through many journeys
and adventures without end,
yet recovered in an instant
on the comet of fleeting memories.

I hold peace in open hands,
the eagle's sudden flight,
the spirited gallop of a foal,
the playfulness of seals.
I am everything that is,
beating, pulsing through my veins.
I hold a world renewed each day
reborn with every step I take...

Beyond

I breathe all that's unseen
- mysteries of time,
silence of stars,
unspoken messages
of winds.

I breathe a universe
compressed in an atom,
- a cosmic abyss
swirling, engulfing
all that is.

My thoughts, - meteors
crossing galaxies unknown -
change the world
ever so subtly,
unrevealed.

With every breath
I find proof of my existence,
- a masterful illusion,
as clear and believable
as a dream?

I breathe fluttering wings,
heavenly hymns,
and Love unfolded
creating, recreating,
all that is...

Seasons of

Grief and Hope

WINTER

AUTUMN

SUMMER

SPRING

New Day

To be a vessel, ready
to be filled, while
never truly holding to its
ever renewed content,

to allow others to swim
in and out our waters,
gladly, freely, at will
down our gentle currents,

to be a painted flower
giving off its perfume
and the joyous hope
of a spring reborn,

to be an empty page
welcoming the writing,
the newness, the challenge
of wisdom and praise

to become soft earth,
smooth, supple, willing,
eager for the molding,
in our Maker's hands,

to offer each breath,
each fleeting precious moment
for the life, for the breath
of this, our fragile world,

and to bless each new day
with the selfless outpouring
of our gifts, of our talents
and our grateful tender love...

PERSONAL REFLECTION

The following are suggestions for personal reflection, journaling or sharing within a group. Artistic expressions may also be useful to express the movements within. Consider making a collage, writing a poem, drawing or painting.

In viewing this journey and reflecting on it:

1) What have I noticed was moved in me?

2) What image or word best describes how I felt?

3) How can I express my inner response to this journey? (drawing, journaling, writing a verse, painting or other)

4) How would I describe the feelings that were stirred? Can I distinguish different feelings?

5) Was there a loss these feelings are linked to? What type of loss was this? What was my relationship to that which I lost?

6) How long ago did this loss occur? Are there any circumstances that make the sadness recur? Are there any other feelings attached to this loss?

7) Where do I perhaps find God, a Higher Power, love, hope and/or meaning in my loss?

8) Is there someone with whom I can share my story?

Bibliography

and

Resources

Bibliography and Resources:

Are, T. L. (1984). *Heaven Knows. Kate.* Connecticut: Morehouse Barlow Co. Inc.

Bertman, S. (1999). *Grief and the Healing Arts. Creativity as Therapy.* New York: Baywood Publishing Co. Inc.

Chittister, J. (2005). *Scarred by Struggle, Transformed by Hope.* Michigan: Eerdmans Publishing Co.

Fitzgerald, H. (1994). *The Mourning Handbook.* New York: Simon & Schuster.

Hill, M. A . *Healing Grief through Art: Art Therapy Bereavement Group Workshops.* http://www.drawntogether.com

Hospice Foundation of America. (2000). Doka, K. *Living with Grief. Children, Adolescents and Loss.* Taylor & Francis Group.

Hospice Foundation of America. (1999). Doka, K. *Living with Grief. At Work, at School, at Worships.* Taylor & Francis Group.

Hospice Foundation of America. (1998). Doka, K. *Living with Grief. Who We Are. How We Grieves.* Taylor & Francis Group.

Hospice Foundation of America. (1997). Doka, K. *Living with Grief. When Illness is prolonged.* Taylor & Francis Group.

Hospice Foundation of America. (1996). Doka, K. *Living with Grief after Sudden Loss. Suicide, Homicide, Accident, Heart Attack, Stroke.* Taylor & Francis Group.

Hospice Foundation of America. (1995). Doka, K. *Children Mourning. Mourning Children.* Taylor & Francis Group.

Jennie, (2007), *Grief, Loss, Recovery. Hope and Health Through Creative Grieving.* http://www.recover-from-grief.com

Kelley, M. (2010). *Grief. Contemporary Theory and the Practice of Ministry*. Minneapolis: Fortress Press.

Kubler-Ross, E. (1969). *On Death and Dying*. New York: McMillan.

Lamers, W. M. (1999). "On the psychology of loss". *Grief and the Healing Arts*. Sandra L. Bertman, New York: Baywood Publishing Co. Inc.

Lewis, C. S. (2001). *A Grief Observed*. New York: Harper Collins Publishers, Inc.

Longaker, C. (1998). *Facing Death and Finding Hope: A Guide to the Emotional and Spiritual Care of the Dying*. New York: Doubleday.

Mitchell, K. & H. Anderson (1983). *All Our Losses, All Our Griefs*. Philadelphia: The Westminster Press.

Miller, J. & Cutshshall, S. (2001). *The Art of Being a Healing Presence*. Indiana: Willowgreen Publishing.

Nullan, S. B. (1994). *How We Die. Reflections on Life's Final Chapter*. New York: Alfred A. Knoff, Inc.

Rando, T. (1991). *How to Go on Living When Someone You Love Dies*. New York: Bantam Books.

Rupp, J. (1990). *Praying Our Goodbyes*. Indiana: Ave Maria Press.

Sullender, R. S. (1999). *Losses in Later Life: A New Way of Walking with God*. New York: Haworth Pastoral Press.

The New American Bible-School and Church Edition. (2000). Kansas: Fireside Bible Publishers.

If you'd like to find out how to contact Monique Cerundolo or when this exhibit will be in display, please go to the website:

https://sites.google.com/site/findinghopeproject/home

Made in the USA
Charleston, SC
12 September 2014